The Say Yes Experience

Get Out of Your Comfort Zone and Into Possibilities

52 Tips to Prevent Burnout and Enhance Your Mental Health

The Say Yes Experience
Published by jessICAREctor Enterprises
jessicarector.com

Copyright © 2024 by Jessica Rector
All rights reserved. Published 2024
Printed in the United States of America

No part of this book may be reproduced or transmitted in any form or by any means without the written permission of the publisher, except in the case of brief quotations.

Except for family and friends, names and identifying characteristics of individuals mentioned have been changed to protect their privacy.

ISBN: 9798327807051

Cover design by: Peter L @okomota
Layout by: solfire@phoenix-farm.com
Cover photo by: Valeria Karpova

Dedication

To my brother, Beastie:
When you unexpectedly passed away, my world turned upside down. It certainly gave me a new perspective on life and how I want to live. This is for you. Thanks for being the first person to ever truly see me and get me.

This is also to you, Reader:
If you've ever felt like you've lost a part of yourself, been too busy to take care of yourself or have put your dreams on hold for someone or something else. This is to ignite your inner, amazing self to live the life you've always wanted.

For B Man:
This whole idea started when you saw me...what I needed and who I wanted to be. Thank you for continually believing in me and pushing me to leap, risk, and ultimately fly outside what I think is possible. You are my greatest gift and biggest blessing.

Table of Contents

Preface 7
Tip 1: What Do You Want? 13
Tip 2: The Say Yes Formula 15
Tip 3: Is It Really Balance? 17
Tip 4: Bring Say Yes to Life 18
Tip 5: Think Small 19
Tip 6: Quick & Easy Is Good 20
Tip 7: What Values Matter 21
Tip 8: Identify Your Values 22
Tip 9: Value Alignment 26
Tip 10: Hack—5 Minute Method 27
Tip 11: Say Yes Bucket List 29
Tip 12: Microstep Bucket List 30
Tip 13: When You Don't Want To 31
Tip 14: 60 Seconds 32
Tip 15: Rewire Your Mind 33
Tip 16: The Real Reasons 34
Tip 17: Negative Thoughts 35
Tip 18: The Stories You Tell 36
Tip 19: Supporting Roles 37

Tip 20: Pushing You 38
Tip 21: The Size of Your Comfort Zone 39
Tip 22: Turn Hard to Easy 40
Tip 23: Say Yes to Yourself 41
Tip 24: The Fun Factor 42
Tip 25: Best Friends 43
Tip 26: Think BIG! 45
Tip 27: Think Small 46
Tip 28: Break it Down 47
Tip 29: Your Daily Life 48
Tip 30: The Three Cs 49
Tip 31: Stay Curious 50
Tip 32: Become Courageous 51
Tip 33: Develop Connections 53
Tip 34: My Mistake 54
Tip 35: Ripple Effect 55
Tip 36: Light Yourself Up 56
Tip 37: Think Less, Act More 57
Tip 38: Start The Domino Effect 58
Tip 39: Let's Go! 59
Tip 40: The Mind Shift 61
Tip 41: The Treadmill 63
Tip 42: Why No? 65
Tip 43: Get Out of Control 66

Tip 44: Bet on You	67
Tip 45: Become a Master	69
Tip 46: Reducing Stress	70
Tip 47: Analyze Paralysis	71
Tip 48: Embracing Change	72
Tip 49: Combating Auto Pilot	73
Tip 50: Say Yes Even When…	75
Tip 51: Fighting for…	76
Tip 52: Lead By Example	79
BONUSES	81
Bonus Tip 1: Say Yes to Yourself	82
Bonus Tip 2: Say Yes to Mental Health	84
Bonus Tip 3: Say Yes to Physical Health	85
Bonus Tip 4: Say Yes to Emotional Health	86
Bonus Tip 5: Say Yes to Adventures	88
Bonus Tip 6: Say Yes to Relationships	89
Bonus Tip 7: Say Yes to Professional Growth	90
Bonus Tip 8: Say Yes to Travel	91
Bonus Tip 9: Say Yes to a Break	92
Bonus Tip 10: Become a Say Yeser	94
MORE	95
ABOUT THE AUTHOR	113

Preface

Saying Yes may seem simple, and in some ways it is.

However, it's also easy to get so caught up with your life that you forget to Say Yes and expand your comfort zone (have you ever ended a year and thought you're in the same place doing the same thing as the year before?).

Maybe you get too in your head about it (what if they don't like me, what if I don't get the promotion, what if my business fails).

Has that ever happened to you?

I've been there myself and know how that can hold you back.

The initial Saying Yes is simple.

The Art of Saying Yes includes follow through and follow up...and that's where it becomes a bit more challenging.

Here's why.

Follow Through: You can Say Yes and even have every intention of doing something, but if you don't take action, then nothing changes.

Not only do you have to Say Yes, but then you need to take immediate action on it. The Say Yes means nothing if it's not attached to an action.

Follow Up: Saying Yes and taking action once is great. Where the magic really happens is in the follow up. Saying Yes, again and again. In fact, it's really magical and will change the trajectory of your life if you Say Yes and take a small action daily. That's where you can really see massive results.

Most people might do it once or twice and then get busy with their days and forget to do it. In order to stay on course, log it in your daily calendar as though it's a meeting with yourself that you can't break.

The more you do it, the better you become at doing it so it becomes a habit. You'll love it so much, you'll soon remember to do it without setting a reminder.

Follow through and follow up are the keys to transformation.

Put your Say Yes in your calendar now for the rest of the week.

Burnout started many years ago for me. Although this book isn't burnout *per se*, it really begins there.

I was healthy (never missing a day of work minus the one day when I was 16 years old and had the flu) and happy, living a great life. I started working for a Fortune 100 company and was their top sales producer, winning every sales award within the first six months of employment. I worked on my days off and extra hours to exceed expectations and goals. I was rockin' it!

So, I worked more, longer, and harder. Leaders were astonished by how I was able to win every award because no one else had done that.

Then something happened.

I was demotivated to go into work. It took everything out of me to have a decent attitude when I got to work. My body wasn't keeping food down. In fact, I was throwing up bile.

I often called in sick to work because I was busy going to the doctor. Many appointments, specialists, and tests later, I'll never forget that day, the doctor said, "We don't know why you're always so sick."

It was discovered I was burned out. When I approached my leaders about it asking for help, resources, and support, they had nothing in place for me and didn't know where I could get what I needed.

I soon left the organization in search of a solution. Several years later, almost the exact same thing happened. Then I realized I needed to create the solution, not to just help myself, but to also help so many others like me that needed help.

I have been keynote speaking, researching, and consulting on burnout for years. Then the pandemic hit. Organizations were finally realizing the importance of addressing and preventing burnout. Yaayy! But I was on the road more than I was home.

When I would get home, I would be exhausted. My young son, B Man, recognized there were parts of me that were lending themselves to burnout, so he said, "Mama, let's Say Yes to stuff."

I thought I was already saying yes to too many things, so I wasn't really keen on saying yes to more. Then he continued, "Let's look for things that light you up, bring you joy, put a smile on your face. Let's stretch you beyond what you think you want to do to find things you may never have thought about. You don't know what can happen or what's possible if you don't try."

I was intrigued and replied, "Yes! Let's do it," and that was my first Say Yes.

What I discovered, uncovered, and explored on our Say Yes Experience journey led to my life transforming and my burnout subsiding. Now I've taught those same lessons and insights to thousands of people.

My hope in sharing them with you throughout this book is that you find value in them to help you in your life—whether you want to prevent burnout, enhance your mental health, stretch your limitations or build your confidence.

We all need some encouragement and a little push from time to time to reach our next level of greatness. If you're reading this, it's your sign to step out of your comfort zone and into possibilities.

The world awaits you, my friend! This is only the beginning. I can't wait to see all the amazingness that's in store for you.

Let's go!

JessICAREctor and Blaise Rector

Tip 1: What Do You Want?

Have you ever really stopped to ask yourself this?

What do I want?

You may think you know what you want or maybe what you want has been decided for you because it's what your parents, partner or kids want, and you don't want to create waves, so you just go along with it.

Or maybe you've never ever considered what you want because you've been doing whatever you're doing however you've been doing it for so long, you've forgotten to ever consider that maybe, just maybe, you now want something different.

So, what do you want?

What do you really want?

It's not just about Saying Yes.

What is Saying Yes anyway?

Saying Yes is about discovering what it is you want...what you *really* want and then Saying Yes to making it happen.

As my good friend, Lisa Rehurek says, "Dreaming big is an equal opportunity," just like Saying Yes it. Everyone can do it, no matter where you are at this point in life, and it's free.

Often, that doesn't mean staying where you are. A Yes means doing something new or in a different way, stretching yourself beyond what you think is possible, then risking more, even a little, in order to get where you want to be.

You likely are saying yes to too many things already. Now it is time for discovering what you're saying yes to and making sure it lines up to what you want. You can't get where you want to go or be who you want to be without knowing what you truly want.

So, what do you want?

If you don't know what you want, you'll likely never get it.

Tip 2: The Say Yes Formula

Saying Yes may seem simple initially, but when you dig a little deeper, there is actually a formula to what happens.

If you just Say Yes, nothing really happens. Nothing changes.

There are two components that make Say Yes so powerful ... alignment and action.

It takes both of them partnering for Say Yes to work. Otherwise, you'll find yourself Saying Yes to things you don't want (we've all been there), which leads you to places you don't want to go or behaving like someone you don't want to be.

ALIGN: This is your life...YOU decide what you want, where you want to be, and how you want to get there. Pause for a moment, think about where you are now and what you're doing—how does it align to what you really want?

ACTION: Then Saying Yes proceeds an action. Without action, you're stagnant. When you verbally Say Yes, an action must follow.

Where do you want to be? And it's okay, if you don't know yet.

Values Align + Action Steps = Saying YES

Tip 3: Is It Really Balance?

You often hear "balance" used about life choices, whereas I think it's more about alignment.

With balance, you will always be teetering and choosing one over the other. At some point, you'll fall because you can't maintain balance forever. It's just not possible, plus it's exhausting. Something will have to give at some point.

With alignment, you don't have to choose. You can have both because they are parallel, are moving in the same direction, and can go on infinitely. They almost feed off each other.

It's the same idea about being an "and" person instead of an "or" person. Do you want cookies or ice cream? I want cookies AND ice cream. Do you want a great career or to be a good parent? I want a great career AND to be a good parent. Don't settle for "or" when you can and should have "AND."

What in your life or work needs alignment?

Tip 4: Bring Say Yes to Life

Action is the key to anything.

An idea will stay an idea without an action behind it.

A dream will remain so until you take action.

A relationship will become stale without action.

Fear will always grow unless you initiate action through that fear.

Action is the catalyst for every habit, bucket list item or change.

You can Say Yes to something in your mind or out loud, but it requires action in order for it to come to life and become your reality. Action is the key to getting anything done, enhancing your mental health and growing in any aspect, whether work, life or relationships.

Nothing exists without action. Action is the key to bringing Say Yes into your reality.

What in your life (whether a habit, a goal or a dream) needs action right now?

Tip 5: Think Small

It's not always about big action, although that can be fun and exciting.

How do you feel when you think of big action or large steps?

If you're like most people, you might feel overwhelmed or stressed with just the idea of the bigness of it. This can lead to burnout That's the last thing we want, because when you feel that way, you can feel stuck and then likely won't do anything.

When you have a big project, goal or Say Yes bucket list item, your brain needs to be able to process the action needed into steps that are manageable, so your brain doesn't shut down. Break down the big into small microsteps.

Then jot down the microsteps you need to take. This allows your brain to recognize each step toward your goal is doable.

Small consistent actions create massive results and prevent burnout.

What is one small action you can take today?

Tip 6: Quick & Easy Is Good

Giant steps can keep you stuck by making you feel overwhelmed, whereas microsteps allow you to get something completed and accomplished fast. When you do this, it creates a win. This keeps you motivated to *want* to keep doing the microsteps, because it will create more wins. And wins feel good.

When you win, your brain says, "Wow! That was quick and easy. I can do that again." So, it works on the next microstep, finishing the next one fast too.

Your brain recognizes how fast and easy it is (because we like fast and easy), so it keeps up the desire to take action.

These microsteps, along with how your brain processes the wins, allows you to make forward progress fast. Consistency with small action is key to achieve goals, dreams, and ambitions.

What's a recent small win you've had?
(Go ahead, write it down, there is no wrong answer.)

_____

Tip 7: What Values Matter

In order to be in alignment, you must first know what matters to you.

Until this point, you might not have given much thought to your core values. Maybe you don't realize what really drives you or why you choose Option A over other choices.

When you know your values, then your decisions, relationships, conversations, and projects all become more manageable.

You'll want to do what aligns with your values because it's easy, fun, and you reach your goals faster.

Things or people that don't align with your values feel hard, time consuming or painful. They feel like work, so you don't want to put the effort into them. They also bring down your morale and crush your motivation to actually perform or interact with them. In order to live in "easier" mode, stay aligned with your values. So first, you must know what they are.

What is one of your core values?

_____

Tip 8: Identify Your Values

You've started by identifying one of your core values.

Depending on life's circumstances, the value you've identified may not come into play with your current goal, so it's vital to identify several of your values.

In situations where multiple values are combating each other, how will you figure out which one outweighs the other?

Let's say two of your values are simplicity and prestige. They might combat each other when you're buying a house. Do you keep it simple with a smaller house or go for prestige with a bigger one?

Knowing which ones are important, and in what order, will make challenges easier to navigate.

On the following pages, you'll find a list of core values. Circle the ones that resonate with you. Then narrow it down to your top 5, in order of most to least important.

Take your time. You may like a lot of them but it's vital to narrow it down to your top 5.

List of Core Values

Accountability	Connection	Flexibility
Achievement	Contentment	Forgiveness
Adaptability	Contribution	Freedom
Adventure	Cooperation	Friendship
Altruism	Courage	Fun
Ambition	Creativity	Generosity
Authenticity	Curiosity	Grace
Balance	Dignity	Gratitude
Belonging	Diversity	Growth
Caring	Efficiency	Happiness
Collaboration	Equality	Health
Commitment	Ethics	Honesty
Community	Excellence	Hope
Compassion	Fairness	Humor
Competence	Faith	Independence
Confidence	Family	Initiative

Integrity	Patience	Success
Joy	Patriotism	Support
Justice	Peace	Teamwork
Kindness	Perseverance	Thoughtful
Knowledge	Persuasion	Tradition
Leadership	Power	Travel
Learning	Pride	Trust
Legacy	Recognition	Truth
Love	Reliability	Serenity
Loyalty	Resilience	Service
Mindfulness	Resourceful	Spirituality
Nature	Respect	Understanding
Openness	Responsibility	Vision
Optimism	Risk-taking	Vulnerability
Order	Sacrifice	Wealth
Organization	Safety	Wisdom
Originality	Security	
Parenting	Stewardship	
Passion	Sympathy	

MY TOP 5 CORE VALUES

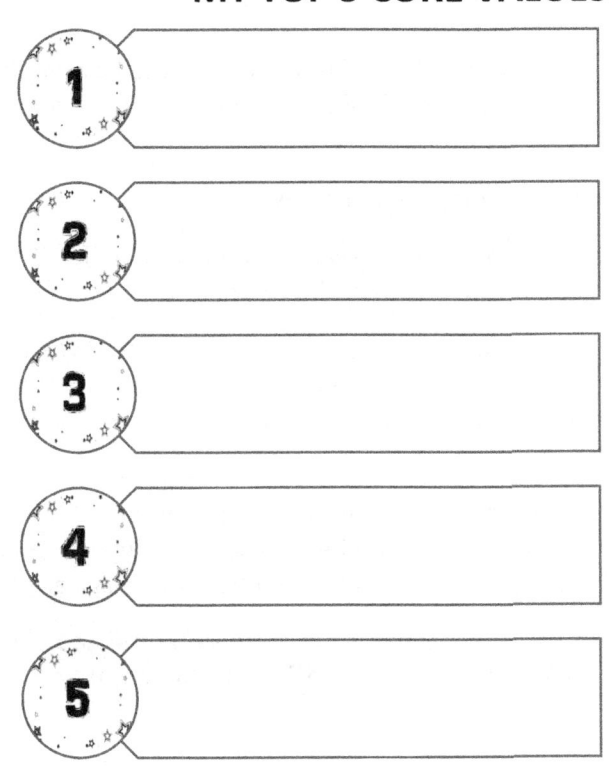

1.

2.

3.

4.

5.

Tip 9: Value Alignment

Now that you have your top five values, review how you're living, working, leading, loving, acting, communicating, showing up in relationships, etc.

You can't change things you're not aware exist.

Pay attention: do your values align in every area of life? If not, what can you adjust so your values lead your behavior?

The more aligned they are, the easier life will be. When they are aligned, it'll be much easier to say, "No. Onto the next," and move on to what better fits with what you want, desire, and need.

Have you ever stayed at a job or in a relationship knowing something didn't feel right, just hoping it would get better? When you live aligned, it's easier to let go when things don't match your values instead of living in the hope that it'll get better or magically change.

Are you living in alignment with your values? If not, what microsteps will help you begin?

_____

Tip 10: Hack—5 Minute Method

When a conversation or situation doesn't go as planned, you might replay it in your head. Again and again.

You tell a friend about it, a colleague and then your spouse. Instead of it taking up a few minutes, it lasts for hours ruining your whole day.

When B Man (my son) and I were on a travel adventure, I had an encounter with a manager at one of the places we visited.

The manager was impolite and rude. He refused to try to understand my point of view.

When we left, I talked to B about it.

Then I rehashed it again to him...and again.

B finally said, "Mom, you have five minutes. That's all I'm giving you, because I don't want you to keep talking about it. You have five minutes to let it go."

Then he shared with this hack he created. Guess what?! It really worked.

It helped me to focus on other things, while allowing me to stay present and in the moment with him (instead of replaying what happened, thinking about the manager who wasn't thinking about me).

Here's a Say Yes hack to quickly work through it and not use brain power to retrace it. B created what we call the 5 Minute Method.

Minute 1: Share, vent or relay what happened

Minute 2: Process it. Think about what was said or happened.

Minute 3: Ask yourself, "What was my part in it?" Be truthful.

Minute 4: What lesson did you learn from the experience.

Minute 5: Let it go!

When you let it go, it frees up space in your brain to focus on more important things in your life.

What situation, conversation or experience can you use this hack on?

Tip 11: Say Yes Bucket List

When you were younger, you had a wish or a dream. Then life got in the way and you might have put it on the back burner or forgotten about it altogether.

Or maybe your dream has changed over the years, but it still burns somewhere inside of you. We all have a dream, even if we seem to forget about it.

Now is the best time to bring it back or the perfect time to start a new one. You can also keep adding items to this list and working towards amazing life experiences. Maybe it's a trip, a particular career or having a once-in-a-lifetime adventure. It might be something simple like connecting with an old friend or reading a bedtime story to a young child.

What is the #1 item on your Say Yes Bucket List?

_____

Tip 12: Microstep Bucket List

To achieve your Say Yes Bucket List, you have to take action.

It might initially seem overwhelming when you think of the change it'll take to turn your Say Yes Bucket List item into realty. So, jot down a microstep to begin the journey.

Once you complete the first microstep, what is the next one you need to take? Maybe it's that same thing done every day for a while or it might be a different action altogether. For example, saving $5/day to afford your trip (same thing done), enrolling in and attending a class (different microsteps) or researching where you want to go or what you want to do (same thing until completed, then on to a new step).

What's one thing you can Say Yes to today to move you one step closer to a bucket list item coming true?

_____

Tip 13: When You Don't Want To

Once you know what your Say Yes Bucket List items are, pick the first one you want to focus on. What is the first thing you need to do to move closer to completing it? Don't think too long and hard about this. Just do something, anything. Then keep the momentum going.

Doing it one time isn't enough. You must take a small action daily, no matter how tiny it is, even on days when you don't want to do it; well, *especially* on those days. Sometimes when a microstep is really small, you might think, "It doesn't matter if I do it." It does matter!

Why? It will move you closer to your goal. Even the smallest action keeps momentum going and you feeling like you're making progress. It makes the next action step just a bit easier to do, and you remember how your brain likes that, don't you?!

Don't stop moving forward. Have it become part of your daily habits and life.

What is something you can do today to move closer to your dream?

Tip 14: 60 Seconds

It's easy to put a small thing off until tomorrow. In fact, you've likely done that before, thinking you don't have time now.

You make time for the things that are important to you, and it's important to keep yourself on track, whether it's for a task, spending time with family, or turning your dreams and bucket list items into reality.

You might have conjured up in your mind that it'll take a lot of time or effort, when in fact, 60 seconds can make a massive difference. Those itty bitty steps often don't take much time.

One minute is all it takes to enhance your mental state and beat burnout by having fun, creating laughter or putting aside $5 for what you want.

The more you do it, you create a habit, then the easier it becomes.

Challenge Yourself:

- → What can you get done in 5 minutes today?
- → What can you get done in even 1 minute?

Tip 15: Rewire Your Mind

Your mind is wired to say no. It'll think of all the ways something won't work out or the things that will go wrong.

It'll think it's too hard, you don't have the money or you don't possess the skills. It'll try to stop you every time.

It's your job to Say Yes, and to say it loud and proud...to not listen to that little voice trying to convince you otherwise because it's just lying to you.

You can do it. It all begins with the belief in yourself, which will grow your confidence, in every area of your life.

You are smart, wise, brave, adventurous. You are a great leader. You have the money (or can find/save the money). You have the skills and the abilities. You have everything you need to get where you want to be, do what you want to do, and be who you want to become.

How can you start believing in yourself so it's easier to Say Yes?

Tip 16: The Real Reasons

When you find yourself saying No, peel back the layers to get to the real reasons behind it. How can you turn it into a Say Yes?

It takes time and work, but it'll be worth it to get to the core issues. When you are aware of the core issues, then you can see how they're impacting your life, where they're showing up in it (in experiences, conversations, situations, relationships), and how they affect you.

Here are some questions to get you started.

- → Why am I thinking this?
- → Do I believe it?
- → Where is it coming from?
- → Who used to tell me this?
- → How is this showing up in other areas of my life?
- → How does it impact me or the situation when it shows up?
- → Who else is impacted by this?
- → What relationships are affected by this thinking?

Tip 17: Negative Thoughts

B Man and I stood on a cliff (some say more of a high platform) looking over the greenest blue ocean I'd ever seen.

When I went to jump off this cliff, my brain stopped me from jumping. Even though I was wearing a life jacket and I could see way down into the clear water, I felt fear—what if the life jacket doesn't work or what if an animal I can't see grabs my leg?

B Man said, "Negative thoughts are creeping in. Don't listen to them." I went to jump off again, pausing before going.

He said, "Mama, you got this. You can do it."

Finally, I jumped off, and he said, "Way to go Mama. You got this. Grab the rope," and then gave me a thumbs up.

The negative thoughts went away when I decided to take action and walk (jump) through the negative to the other side.

What negative thoughts are hindering you from Saying Yes? What action do you need to take in order to work your way through them?

Tip 18: The Stories You Tell

When you're aware you have negative thoughts, you are more mindful of how and when they show up. Then you have the ability to stop them in their tracks. When you don't, they take on a sneaky life of their own, creating stories that can last your whole life.

Some of those stories started when you were a child. For instance, the story of not being smart enough often starts in children if they are compared to their siblings or classmates, or don't get the grades expected of them.

Eventually, they tell themselves the story that they are not smart, which over time turns to, "I'm dumb." Of course they think, I can't figure that out…or no wonder why it takes me longer to do it because I'm dumb. As they grow, that becomes the story they repeat to themselves in various situations, even when it doesn't seem related.

These stories will impact your mental health and keep you from Saying Yes.

What story are you telling yourself? How can you reframe the story to help you Say Yes?

Tip 19: Supporting Roles

We all have stories we tell ourselves that aren't true. The key is to:

   a) recognize the stories you tell yourself
   b) stop the stories as soon as you start to tell them
   c) have a great support system to remind you the story is a lie

When I was jumping off the cliff, B Man was a great support. He lovingly and gently called me out reminding me the negative thoughts were stopping me.

He supported me...sharing with me that I could do it, and that he believed in me.

After I did it, he encouraged me, "Way to go Mama. You got this. Grab the rope!" He gave me a thumbs up that I did a good job.

Surround yourself with strong supporters. They're vital to all of us for growing, thriving, and Saying Yes, which builds confidence and eradicates your limiting beliefs.

Who is your support? Who can you ask to better support you?

Tip 20: Pushing You

Is your support person someone who always agrees with you?

It's nice to have people in your life who encourage and cheer you on. It's also imperative to have someone, at least one person, in your life who pushes you--who gently nudges you outside your comfort zone—that person who won't agree with you just to pacify you or who will share another perspective or insight.

You need that in order to grow and flourish into the best version of yourself.

If you always want someone to agree with you, look in the mirror. That person always will. If you want to thrive, find someone who kindly pushes you past limitations or helps eliminate any doubt.

That is the person who will guide you to new heights, refuse to let you play small, and believes in you when you don't see it in yourself.

Who in your life pushes you beyond what you think is possible?

Tip 21: The Size of Your Comfort Zone

Take a look at your comfort zone. If you had to measure it, would you say it's small, medium or large?

If it's small, you like routines. Yet, if you stay locked in a few routines, you are less likely to reach your dream, goals or ambitions. If it's small, when something scares you (or an idea scares you), you likely say No and never change your mind.

If it's medium, you find yourself trying "new" every now and then or attempting something small. If it doesn't work out or if it's too hard, you go back to your normal ways fast.

If it's large, you may thrive on risk. You're willing to put yourself out there, maybe just to see if you can do it and succeed. You don't shy away from new thoughts or adventures. In fact, you might thrive on those.

The smaller your comfort zone is, the more confined you are. The more you stretch it, the more freedom you have to truly be you.

What is one (small) way you can stretch your zone today?

Tip 22: Turn Hard to Easy

When something doesn't come easily we label it "hard." Then we repeat it.
- → "I don't want to do it; it's hard."
- → "It's going to take me too long, because it's hard."

The more you say it's hard, the more your brain believes that to be true, so the less it will do it. Instead say:
- → "I got this."
- → "I have the skills to do this."
- → "This comes easy to me."

This tricks your brain into believing those are true. Then you'll turn what you once thought was impossible into probable. How? You'll turn the impossible to possible by telling yourself it's easy. When something is easy, you'll take one microstep to make it happen. With each microstep, it becomes probable (the chance of it turning into your reality increases with every microstep you take). You just turned the impossible into probable because you believed it was easy and took microsteps to make it happen.

What did you once think was hard that over time became easy?

Tip 23: Say Yes to Yourself

Need an idea for a starting place? The first thing you can turn from hard to easy is to Say Yes to yourself!

What lights you up and brings you joy?

Maybe it's something you thought you'd get back to or a dream you've forgotten about. It might be an idea you had that you've put off because you've been busy caring for your family or a sick parent or you're in a stable career because it's what your family (or you) needed at the time but it doesn't fulfill you.

Yet there is a lingering in your heart and in your soul. Something in you wants more...you were meant for more, whether it's to ignite the travel bug, start your own business, end a heartbreaking relationship or explore the courage to start a new one.

What makes your soul sing and your heart beat faster?

The best way to enhance your mental health and prevent burnout is to Say Yes to you! Put yourself on the plate and live the life you love.

Tip 24: The Fun Factor

When you feel stressed, overwhelmed or burned out (and who doesn't these days), the first thing you take out of your days is fun, yet it's the #1 thing you need to combat these feelings.

Work and fun aren't mutually exclusive. The more fun people have at work, the more they want to work at that place. Start having a culture of fun: at work and at home.

Let loose, laugh more, experience joy.

It doesn't have to take long. Let your brain explore the different ways you can have fun in five minutes or in just 60 seconds. Ask family, friends, and colleagues. Ya'll will come up with some of the best answers, and just this exercise alone may produce some belly laughs.

When you incorporate more fun, you build a stronger team dynamic, better communication, and more happiness. It's a win-win.

Where can you incorporate more fun into your day?

_____

Tip 25: Best Friends

I've never been a big dog person. I know, I know. Hear me out.

I grew up with a few small dogs, but as an adult, it was never my desire or longing to have a dog or any pet. Yet B Man has said for many years, "Mama, I want a brother or a dog."

The man has yet to come around for the brother, so I finally gave into a dog...well a puppy, because B Man only wanted a puppy, so they could grow up together.

It was a HUGE adjustment at first, and in some ways, it still is (hello messes, chewing, and jumping), but what I've found is our dog, Shadow (aka Brother), has also brought so much joy, fun, and laughter to our lives. Plus, B Man now has a playmate and someone else to snuggle with.

Sometimes the thing that makes the biggest difference in your life is Saying Yes to something you never thought you'd Say Yes to, but that ends up being what you need most in life.

What can you Say Yes to that will greatly enhance your life?

I saw a video on social media from DadAdvicefromBo, Part 7.

His daughter has a brain injury, and because of all the pain she has endured, she didn't want to live anymore.

He hated to see her in so much agony. As a last resort, he got her a dog...and everything changed. She started playing with the puppy, smiling more, laughing and cuddling with the dog.

She has never mentioned again not wanting to live because now (I think) she has something or someone to live for. When you feel sad or lonely, Say Yes to you...whether it's finding someone that brings you joy or something that makes you smile.

Finding and having something or someone to live for literally changes your life. It fills your heart in ways you never expected.

Check out DadAdvicefromBo on social.

He has some amazing content and his videos are extremely helpful.

Tip 26: Think BIG!

Remember when you were a child and you had those grand, big ideas? Your imagination went wild with what was possible. If anyone told you it wasn't possible, you vehemently disagreed.

You could have this career. You would study that. You could create it. You would do anything your brain could imagine.

Tap into those big dreams and grand ideas.

Now think **bigger.** Expand your mind beyond what you think is possible.

That, my friend, is the only way Google, Apple, Amazon or Walmart came to be. Or how the car or an airplane was created.

When someone thought, "What would happen if..." They dared to imagine what could be and then expanded on it to create our current reality. (They took action steps to make the thought a reality.)

Think, explore, dare, dream.

Turn it from just something to think about into your reality. *What is your big, big Say Yes dream?*

Tip 27: Think Small

I know, I know. I just encouraged you to think big, and now I'm suggesting you think small.

Sometimes BIG feels overwhelming, so it's important to remind yourself you can also think small and still be taking action.

Some of the small things you might forget about or think you'll do them tomorrow. Then you find tomorrow never comes. Years pass, and you still aren't doing them.

Whether catching the latest movie, reaching out to an old friend or going out on a date...when you're busy, those small things can make a massive difference to you and others you care about.

Make a list of the small things you want to do. Then carve out the time it takes and do one a week. You'll relish the feeling you get from finally doing it as well as the joy that fills you.

Start really small, if you must. Ride a bike, go to a pool or try a new ice cream parlor.

What is the first small thing on your list?

Tip 28: Break it Down

Doesn't that title make you want to (break) dance?! When you're faced with something big, whether it's a project at work, a challenging conversation or a goal, break it down.

Big things can feel stressful and then you can get analysis paralysis. This is where you think about it from every angle then don't do anything because you keep thinking and thinking and thinking and striving for a totally perfect answer.

Take the project and break it down into microsteps, those small actions. What is the first thing you need to do begin the project?

Start small, and you'll get traction. Then use that to do the next small step and the next. Before you know it, you'll be using that momentum to make progress on your project and finish it.

If you just keep looking at the whole picture, you'll stay in stagnation, feeling stuck and overwhelmed. Prevent burnout by breaking it down.

What is the first microstep you can take today to move closer to your goal and desired outcome?

Tip 29: Your Daily Life

Saying Yes is a choice. Instead of doing the same things in the same ways, find a new adventure or experience. Explore a new path or journey.

Then uncover ways to Say Yes each day. It could be with a new recipe, stopping work at 5 pm, trying a different genre of book or discovering a new board game.

The more you Say Yes, the easier it becomes. With each Yes that meshes with your values and goals, you stretch yourself. You examine ideas you would have never thought about. You find ways to have more fun or invite more joy into your life. You let yourself have more freedom.

Saying Yes is really a mindset that you should implement into your daily life. The more you allow your mind to be open to the "other" or "another," the more life you'll be exploring and living.

What can you Say Yes to that incorporates a new mindset and way of living into your daily life? Imagine more smiles, joy and happiness coming your way. That's what's in store for you!

Tip 30: The Three Cs

Saying Yes sparks the three Cs: curiosity, courage, and connection.

These three might not be things you think about often, but they are vital to every aspect of your life.

Curiosity allows you to learn, gain a new perspective or develop in any area.

Courage leads to being bolder, whether in your relationships, in the boardroom or facing your biggest fears.

Saying Yes forms stronger bonds and relationships, which leads to deeper connection in yourself and with others.

The key component to Saying Yes is being intentional. That you're not just getting through today to get on to tomorrow and then the next day. You want to be intentional and present in every day, so you can actively thrive and not just survive.

Before we take a deeper dive into these three core elements, think about which ones needs your focus or attention.

Tip 31: Stay Curious

Young kids ask, "Why?" a lot. Why is the sky blue? Why don't people fly? Why is it called that?

As we get older, we lose this sense of adventure and curiosity, yet it's that curiosity that helps us solve problems, better understand our world, and build stronger connections.

When you ask questions, you learn and grow. You form a deeper understanding which evokes more compassion and empathy. Saying Yes ignites curiosity in yourself, places, and events. It sparks more insight, innovation and creativity, which can transform the world.

When you're learning about someone, ask questions. When you're needing to solve a problem, ask questions. When you want to help someone, ask questions.

It's not just about asking questions, ask better questions too.

Questions often are the solution to whatever challenge you're facing.

Where and to whom can you ask better questions?

Tip 32: Become Courageous

We all have fears. They start off super small, and when you don't take action, you allow the fear to control you.

The more time that passes, the bigger that fear becomes, then the less likely you are to do anything about it.

So, it's not about facing your fears, it's about breaking through them.

When you Say Yes, you break through the fear to something amazing that waits for you on the other side...Your greatness.

Your greatness, your next level, your potential will never be reached as long as you allow fear to control you. It's time to take back your power and take action through your fear.

Each time you Say Yes to a fear, you're also building your confidence. The more confidence you possess, the more fearless you become.

My friend, you are here for so much more, but you're allowing a fear to control you.

The fear of rejection, that you'll make a mistake or fail, you'll get hurt, you won't be liked, can't get the job, you'll be judged, aren't smart/pretty/funny enough or whatever else you're telling yourself.

It's time to break through this fear and conquer it.

You can do anything you want.

You can achieve anything you desire.

It's time to break through this fear, be courageous, and build your confidence along the way. Then, my friend, you'll be unstoppable!

Now is your time to shine, to let the world truly see who you are.

Be bold.

Be brave.

Be courageous!

The world is waiting!

How can you be more courageous and Say Yes?

Tip 33: Develop Connections

In a world where we are constantly connected through devices, it's also a time where we feel the most disconnected and isolated.

You go on social media to connect but don't feel truly connected to others, especially when you compare your life to theirs (it's human nature to do but it can be detrimental and debilitating if you let it).

When you Say Yes, you form a deeper connection with yourself. You find out what you're capable of (and you're capable of sooo much more than you think) and uncover that you're the only one holding you back from anything you desire.

You tap into various layers of yourself, getting to know yourself on a deeper level.

Whether it's your child, spouse, partner, friend or a colleague you might bring along on a Say Yes Experience, you form a stronger relationship, because you're creating a worthwhile experience with them, while also developing lasting memories. Your bond flourishes in the midst of these transformational experiences.

How can you develop stronger connections with yourself and others?

Tip 34: My Mistake

In everything you do, whether in a relationship, at a task or in a role, be mindful of how you're utilizing your skills.

You're likely only using a fraction of your potential. What would happen if you used your full potential?!

You'd reach the next level. You'd achieve your goal faster. You'd become more enlightened, wiser. You'd become a different, better version of yourself.

No matter where you are or what you're doing, there is always something to be studied and learned.

You learn more from mistakes and failures than you ever learn from success. Look at the last mistake you made.

What did you learn from it? How can you use that experience to do or be better next time? To improve upon your habits?

_____

Tip 35: Ripple Effect

With every Say Yes, you grow. You stretch yourself, and when you do that, your comfort zone gets bigger and bigger.

You expand possibilities so that what was once scary or intimidating feels like second nature. Then you use those experiences to teach it and share it with others through your positive stories of perseverance, determination or willpower.

They become inspired to do the same in their lives...and your ripple effect begins.

Wherever you are, there is someone higher on the ladder who you can learn from to continue growing and developing. There is also someone on the ladder below you who can use your guidance and insight to get to where you are.

Ask for help from those higher up the ladder while offering your mentorship to those below you.

Who can you ask to help you and who can you mentor now?

Tip 36: Light Yourself Up

It might take time to get used to Saying Yes to yourself and finding the things that light you up. When you're going, doing, and being for others for so long, you've trained your brain to think in that way. You have to rewire it for you (it's not selfish--it's a necessity--you can't keep going, doing, and being for others without first taking care of yourself).

You might not know where to start, especially if it's been so long since you've put yourself on the plate. You can begin by narrowing your focus down into what you know it's not.

When I was in college, I didn't know what I wanted to major in, but I could tell you what I didn't want to major in (accounting, finance, choir). That was a great place to start, because eventually, I figured out what I did want for a major (marketing).

The same principle applies here. Start the process now.

What is one thing that doesn't light you up or bring you joy?

It'll bring you closer to what does.

Tip 37: Think Less, Act More

It's not just about Saying Yes. You could Say Yes to something and never do it. Then where does that leave you? Right where you still are.

It takes Saying Yes and then taking action on what you're Saying Yes to in order to achieve the desired results you want.

The first part of the formula is to Say Yes.

The second part is to **take an action right after** you Say Yes.

Don't wait. The longer you wait to do it, the more you think about it, and the less likely you are to do it.

Say Yes, then take immediate action. No matter how small the action is, take action right away. You'll feel empowered and energized which will help you take another action and another. That momentum will thrust you into a mental shift to keep going.

What did you Say Yes to today?

What immediate action do you need to now take?

Tip 38: Start The Domino Effect

If you're unsure what you want to Say Yes to, it keeps you from reaching your next level and your potential.

You might feel there are so many things you want to do, so you don't know where to begin. You can always change your focus later.

They key is...just start. There is no right place to start, just begin.

The fun part is once you begin, you'll have so much fun and learn amazing things about yourself that you won't want to stop. You'll keep adding more items to your Say Yes List, which is fantastic.

One idea will spur another and another. Your list will be so long that you'll want to make time to do things on it every week because the more success you'll find and the more joy you'll experience. Keep adding to the list as you go.

The world is waiting.
So which item will ignite your domino effect?

_____

Tip 39: Let's Go!

If you're hesitant to take immediate action, there's a simple way to do this.

You might have heard of Mel Robbins' 5 Second Rule. Before that became popular, I was teaching others The Power of 3 Seconds.

Here's how it works. Think of a runner on the starting line for a race. On your mark, get set, go. And the body automatically shifts into gear to start running.

Why? The idea is something we've been taught since we were kids.

Get ready, get set, ***GO!***

Even as a toddler, your parents held your tiny hands around their index fingers. Stood you up to walk for the first time. Then said, "Ready, Set, Go," as they gently removed your hands from their fingers. And you probably fell. They did it again in the exact same way, "Ready, Set, Go." This happened dozens of times before you might have taken your very first steps, and even more for you to finally walk several feet on your own. This method is engrained in your brain.

The Power of 3 Seconds works the same way. When you're hesitant to take action, say to yourself, "1, 2, 3" or "Ready, Set, Go." Since your brain is wired to move on Go, your body will get into action.

Try it now. What action do you want to take? Want to go for a walk? Say "Ready, Set, Go" and then put on your shoes. Once your shoes are on, it becomes much easier to get out the door or your walk. Putting on your shoes was the microstep toward the goal of taking a walk.

Want to write a book? Start a new document and type one sentence. The next sentence gets easier. Want to start dating? Create a profile on a dating app. Any dating app. Just put yourself out there...and don't think too much about the pictures (yes, put a little thought into it; not much time). It'll never be perfect. Good enough works in this situation, just be honest with the information.

You can think about things so much that nothing gets done. You will overanalyze and talk yourself out of doing it because you don't know how or the best method or who will buy or a slew of other things.

Get out there and do your best and be your best and that, my friend, is ALL that matters. You'll attract the job, person, money, friends that you're supposed to attract.

Tip 40: The Mind Shift

When you've created a habit, your actions are on auto pilot; you do something without giving much thought to it.

Think of taking a shower. You don't think of every single move you make in the shower. You don't consciously think about moving your arm towards the soap, then opening your hand, using your fingers to clutch the soap. Bending your elbow and moving your arm back to put the soap on your skin.

If you thought about every single move, your brain would be worn out five minutes after you woke up. Being on autopilot can be really good in these situations. However, being on autopilot can also be a detriment because it means that you're not actively thinking about the bad habits you have which keep you feeling stuck or stagnant.

You see, my friend, you're here for soooo much more, for so many great things. Some of the habits you have in place are keeping you from fulfilling those amazing things. So, it's time to create a mind shift around some of the things in your life. Instead of thinking and doing things the same way you've always thought or done, **it's time to shake things up.**

If you've always gone the same way to work, take a different route. If you tend to arrive late to events, start getting ready earlier. If you visit the same restaurants, go out on the same night each week or travel to the same places, change it up.

Shifting your mind around what you do and how you do it will expand the possibilities in your life. How?

You find yourself learning more, meeting people you wouldn't have otherwise met or growing your mind, relationships, business or self.

It's time to get unstuck. Feel the excitement of something you never thought you'd do somewhere you've only dreamed of. Relish the thrill of doing it by yourself and the rush of pride when you look back at what you were able to accomplish along the way.

Exude joy when you discover things about yourself you didn't know existed or maybe forgot about them. Take the time to shift your mind on what you think you know and become an avid learner about places, people, cultures, perspectives, and stories.

Ask questions, stay curious, be adventurous, sail away from the shallows and out into the ocean.

Discover. Uncover. Explore.

Tip 41: The Treadmill

You may feel resistance at first. When something is new, that's completely normal. To hesitate. To question. To have that little voice wondering if you should or could or would. Don't let resistance stop you. Recognize it's part of the process, especially when you're on your way to a breakthrough or to something bigger.

I've never been much of an exerciser. It never sounds like fun. Since fun is one of my core values, I tend to shy away from things that don't fit the definition.

B Man wanted to borrow my mom's treadmill to start working out. When we first got the treadmill, I found it ironic how each time he was on the treadmill, I would find myself sitting at the kitchen table eating a bowl of ice cream (my favorite dessert).

A couple months later, I was experiencing some uncertainty with a guy I was dating (if you've been in the dating world recently, you might relate), so I got on the treadmill for a total of 25 minutes.

But every day I changed it slightly. At first, I increased the intervals by only one minute. Then one time, I said, "One more minute." After that minute, I pushed more. At first, my legs could feel the resistance, and I wanted to stop. Then I went the next minute and the resistance was gone. I was able to go from a 5-minute jog to 13 minutes by pushing through the initial resistance. This meant several things:

1. I wasn't pushing myself enough initially. I was doing the minimum to get it done
2. I could accomplish more than I thought without much more effort
3. The resistance existed, but when I pushed past it, I found I was capable of so much more

How much more could I accomplish if I put my mind to it? The same can be said for almost anything.

When you're stretching your body or your mind, you'll initially feel resistance; once you push past it, there's more amazingness on the other side. But often times, as soon as we feel resistance, we stop. We think, "It won't/can't/shouldn't work," so we convince ourselves it won't. Yet, if you decide to push through, like I did exercising, you'll find you haven't hit your stride. You've barely scratched the surface.

Whatever comes your way, when you experience resistance, push a little more, a bit deeper, and you'll find the juicy magic that awaits. Where have you felt resistance recently? Be mindful to not push too much so that it leads to burnout.

Tip 42: Why No?

When an opportunity presents itself, why do you say no?

Dig deep. The answer will empower you.

There's a lot of power in knowing why you say no (instead of yes) to an opportunity (it might be disguised as something else).

Do you believe you're not enough or that you don't have enough time, money, energy, skills, smarts? Maybe you think it requires too much effort (mental, emotional, physical)?

Those are all stories you tell yourself that aren't true.

When you want something bad enough, you can obtain it (asking for help, finding a better job, taking a class, getting a mentor).

What is your excuse for saying no and what will it take for you to Say Yes instead?

Note: Almost everything is an opportunity. Even challenges, issues and struggles are opportunities to problem solve, learn a lesson or grow.

Tip 43: Get Out of Control

When you feel like you don't have control over situations, outcomes or how people will respond, you tend to say no.

No to doing it, no to trying, no to asking, no to problem solving, no to taking the next step…because you want to stay in control. Being in control feels comfortable because it's predictable.

When you're unsure, it can feel chaotic because you're giving control over to something or someone else, and then you have to wait to see how it plays out. Instead of shutting down and giving into the no, Say Yes.

When you Say Yes, you might worry that things could get out of control. You're trying something new and aren't sure what to expect, but that's also part of the fun and excitement that comes with Saying Yes. Something better than what you imagine can take place, you achieve goals faster, form deeper relationships or reach more success.

Saying Yes is about releasing control and embracing the unknown. *What can you Say Yes to and release control over?*

Tip 44: Bet on You

When you Say Yes, it allows you to bet on yourself.

One question I'm asked often is what's led to my success. My consistent answer is, "I always bet on myself." Everyone in the room can be telling me no, but I can confidently stand in front of the room and say, "Yes," because I will always bet on me.

That doesn't mean I have all the answers or know how to do everything. What it does mean is I will find the answers, ask for help or become resourceful in figuring things out. It may not work out the way I plan, but I always learn something from it that helps me grow and flourish in creating future progress and the next steps.

So bet on yourself! Bet on you to know what you need.

Bet on you to follow your dreams and make them happen.

Bet on you that love will happen when it's supposed to.

Bet on you to reach success in all you do.

What will it take for you to start betting on you!

No matter what others say. Have confidence in yourself, your skills, abilities, and know how.

Risk.

In order to get the reward, you have to be willing to take a risk. Every bet has some risk. Calculate it.

Your heart can handle it.

You're smarter than you think. You're more talented than you realize. You're stronger than you believe.

You have everything you need to take the next steps. To move forward. To make massive progress.

Every night, you, my friend, have to look at yourself in the mirror and like who you are and what you see.

If you don't bet on yourself and believe in you, then others won't either.

When things are in despair, know in the depths of your heart and soul, that YOU GOT THIS! You are here for much, much bigger things.

Say Yes to you, and you'll figure out the rest!

Tip 45: Become a Master

Challenges, struggles, and issues are part of life. Instead of seeing them as problems, as "hard," view them as opportunities to Say Yes.

There may be grief, pain or sadness. I encourage you to take the time to process those feelings since they are vital for moving forward.

Once you've given yourself the space and grace to process those, where do the opportunities lie for lessons learned and the chance to move forward?

Even in challenges, there are opportunities.

Opportunities for improvement. Opportunities for you to look at what your part was in what happened. Opportunities to not repeat the same situation. Opportunities to do better next time.

As you look for opportunities, you become a master at seeing them. Then they become easier to take advantage of.

What current challenge could be an opportunity for you?

Tip 46: Reducing Stress

When you have too much work, not enough time or a long To Do list, you might feel overwhelmed or burned out, whether from work, parenting, or caregiving.

When you Say Yes, it allows your brain to think about something besides the things stressing you out. You begin to focus on the activity, experience or situation, especially if it's something you have never done.

You might feel hesitant or nervous Saying Yes, and those feelings can easily overtake your thinking, essentially distracting your brain.

One of the best ways to relieve stress is to have more fun.

Saying Yes gives you the opportunity to invite more fun into your life, whether it's through an adventure, expanding your comfort zone or creating. **Fun is the best medicine for stress.**

What can you Say Yes to in order to reduce stress and increase your fun??

_____

Tip 47: Analyze Paralysis

Are you like me? You think and then think some more. Always striving for the perfect solution. You can over analyze anything, then you are less likely to take action.

I get it. I've been known to do the same thing. What I've discovered is when I Say Yes, it broadens my thinking and helps the analyzing stop.

Why? When you Say Yes, you then take an action which stops analyzing in its tracks.

Saying Yes broadens your thinking and expands your mind beyond what you believe is possible.

It eradicates limitations you've set for yourself.

Analyzing only paralyzes you when you start to repeat any aspects of it on the same problem. Saying Yes expands your possibilities.

Whether in a relationship, conversation or new project, *what have you analyzed and how can you Say Yes to take action* and stop the analyze paralysis in the future?

Tip 48: Embracing Change

Change happens. So does resistance to change.

You get comfie doing the same things in the same way in the same environment with the same people.

When a new leader is hired, you're tasked with a different project or a relationship dissolves, the change can be painful, especially when it's unexpected.

Instead of resisting the change, create a mind shift around it. Stop thinking of all the "bad" things that can happen because of it.

Start seeing it as an opportunity. A chance for things to be better, improved or enhanced. After all, you don't know if it will be good unless you give it a go. If it turns out poorly, easy peasy...just move on to another step.

So instead of fighting change, embrace it. Say Yes to change and all the unexpected amazing things that are waiting for you because it just might be what your heart, soul and you need most (you just didn't know it). *What change has recently happened that you can begin to embrace and Say Yes to?*

Tip 49: Combating Auto Pilot

You're busy. Your days are full of working, cleaning, laundering, activiting, partnering, parenting, cooking, and so much more.

You get in a routine so you don't have to actively think, just get things done faster (and maybe to keep going from one thing to the next without losing energy).

Yet, because of these routines, you forget to actively engage or think—your brain is on auto pilot. The days quickly pass by, as do months and years. What would happen if you started actively thinking throughout your day? Instead of being on auto pilot for the whole day, you think "What do I want to...(do, be, make, create, develop)?"

Start with something super little, maybe something that might even seem insignificant at first glance like taking out a puzzle and putting it on a table or ordering a book.

Tomorrow, put two pieces of the puzzle together. Read the first page of that new book. Set that as your goal to do each day....two pieces of the puzzle—the next page of the book.

Small. Simple. Doesn't take much time. In fact, it'll take less than five minutes.

What you'll find is that after a few days, you'll put four pieces of the puzzle together or read two pages of the book. After a week, you'll be putting 10 pieces together or reading 4 pages of the book. Then before you know it, the puzzle will be done and the book will be read.

Those things that seem too small and almost insignificant are the exact things you need to be doing right now to Say Yes to less busyness, to get out of auto pilot and into your brain. To decompress and recharge.

Puzzling and reading are activities that light your brain up because they get it thinking again. The exact thing you need to combat being on auto-pilot and rejuvenating yourself.

When you Say Yes to brain activity, your brain wants to keep being active. Then you'll overflow with brilliant ideas to develop.

What small, insignificant activity will you choose to begin this empowering change?

Tip 50: Say Yes Even When...

On The Say Yes Experience podcast, my guest, Lisa, was offered a project, but she had never done anything like it before.

Your inclination might be to say no, since you don't know *how* to do it. Lisa, however, Said Yes to it!

She planned to figure it out, and figure it out she did. She exceeded expectations, even her own, and it led to more projects she was in charge of and a job offer. All because she Said Yes.

Don't wait until you know how to do something before you Say Yes. You're resourceful. You're smart. You're wise. You can and will figure it out along the way. Bet on you!

Go out and have fun, you can figure out the relationship. Sell the product, then figure out how to make it. Apply for the promotion, then figure out what to say in the interview.

What can you Say Yes to and then figure it out as you go?

Because something amazing waits on the other side of Say Yes.

Tip 51: Fighting for...

What is the story you've told yourself since you were a kid?

That you're not lovable? That you don't get what you want? That you don't have the experience?

In what specific way do you feel you're not good enough? Now rethink it with your adult brain.

Those stories are lies. They come from what someone else thought or said to you. Over time, you believed them to be true.

And they aren't.

You are lovable. You deserve what you want. You have experience.

You're an amazing person who is destined for much greatness. The only thing stopping you from it is yourself.

What will it take for you to believe in yourself and to fight for what you believe and what you want?

You may think it's hard. It's not.

It's easy.

All it takes is not caring what other people think about you. That means to stop giving weight to their opinion and allowing it to outweigh what you know about yourself to be true.

Want the job? Go apply for it.

Want to find the love of your life? Start dating.

Desire to build a dream life? Begin with one goal.

The decision to be your best self is easy. Then it's just about taking small, consistent action. There will be days you don't want to do something, well my friend, do it anyway.

You don't want to send out 25 emails? Do it anyway.

You would rather eat ice cream than run on the treadmill? Run anyway.

You want someone to knock on your door and ask you out? Go on a dating app anyway.

Whatever you want, be willing to take the steps to get there.

You've been too concerned about what other people will say or think. Who cares. The truth is they don't think about you anyway.

You're here to live *your* life, because it's your life.

Tip 51: Continued ... Fighting For ...

On The Say Yes Experience Podcast, my guest, Steve, was diagnosed with cancer. Instead of sitting down, he fought for his life. In the midst of chemotherapy, when most people can't move much, he competed in Ironmans. He fought for his life and he's alive and thriving because of it.

So fight for what you want.

Fight for what you believe.

Fight for what you deserve and don't stop fighting until you get it.

Who do you need to stop listening to?

_____

What are you willing to fight for?

_____

Tip 52: Say Yes to Leading by Example

You're leading by example, whether at work or home. When you Say Yes, you're encouraging others to Say Yes.

They may witness you Saying Yes and then it not working out or you failing a particular Say Yes. That's okay. We aren't trying to portray Saying Yes as perfection.

You take risks when you Say Yes, and that's part of the experience. If you don't risk, you won't be able to enjoy the reward.

Others will also witness you Saying Yes, and it leading to extraordinary experiences, situations, and relationships. It will motivate and inspire them to Say Yes in their own lives because whether it leads to amazing experiences or lessons learned, people will want to be a part of it for themselves.

They will incorporate Say Yes into their lives, then it leads to a massive ripple effect, all because you're showing up as your best self by Saying Yes.

How can you Say Yes more and lead by example in all areas of life?

Bonuses

Bonus Tip 1: Say Yes to Yourself

You are the last thing on your plate.

You keep going, doing, and being for everyone and everything else, and somehow forget about yourself in the process.

Then you get up the next day, and do it all over again. Never thinking about what you need or what.

It's time to change all of that. It's not a luxury to take care of yourself; it's a necessity.

If you want to go, do and be for others by helping with tasks and projects, you MUST first take care of you.

Right now, in this moment, what do you need? A vacation? Bath? Relaxation? Massage? Time alone? A walk down the street or in the park? Someone to do laundry and the dishes?

Yes, these are short term ideas to help yourself. If you've been putting yourself off a long time, which I'm sure you have, then these are some great places to start.

They won't resolve overwhelm or burnout (that's a whole 'nother book 🙂), but they will help you feel better in the moment. Sometimes this moment is all you have for the day.

Take advantage of it. And make sure you carve out more time for yourself tomorrow and every addition day.

Start where you are with what you have. What do you need right now?

How can you keep giving to yourself, even if it's only for five minutes a day?

Because sometimes five minutes can make the difference between a breakdown and a break through, and you should take what you can get when you can get it.

Carve out time for yourself daily.

You need it, and you deserve it.

It's also the only way you'll be able to keep going, doing, and being. After all, if not for you, everything else wouldn't be able to operate the way it does.

You are needed!

Bonus Tip 2: Say Yes to Mental Health

Your mental health is the foundation of everything you do and everything you don't do. Yet often times it's the last thing you think about, if you think about it at all.

Saying Yes to your mental health is a great place to start, because when your mental health is impacted, it affects everything else in your life (good or bad). What is currently impacting your mental health?

Here are a few ways to Say Yes to your mental health:

→ **Journaling**—write in a lovely journal your ideas, goals or dreams. Start or end your days this way.
→ **Gratefulness**—jot down three things you're grateful for. This keeps you in the present and not thinking of the past or future, which can lead to stress or overwhelm.
→ **Breathing**—take a few deep breaths and release them slowly. As you take them, solely focus on your breathing and not the worries of the day.

Bonus Tip 3: Say Yes to Physical Health

When you think of working out, you may think you need to do it six days a week, two hours a day. What does that feel like? Work, and hard work to most of us. So, you just don't want to do it. After all, who wants to work even more than they already do?!

Instead of thinking of physical activity as working out, create a mind shift to view it as Saying Yes to more movement. When you move your body, it activates your mind to move too, creating more energy, ideas, and creativity. Say Yes to a walk midday, stretching your body or dancing to your favorite song. If your favorite song doesn't make you want to dance, I encourage you to get a new favorite song. ☐

Whether it's for 20 minutes or only 2 minutes, get up and move your body. Your body and mind will thank you for it.

Get into action now. How will you add more movement to your day?

Bonus Tip 4: Say Yes to Emotional Health

One minute our emotions can be in check and the next minute, they are out of whack, especially with so much stress, overwhelm and burnout impacting our daily lives. Let's face it, the world out there is not easy to handle.

It's vital to check in with yourself each day about how you're feeling and doing. You get caught up in being busy and getting through the day, you don't regularly check in with your emotions.

So how are you feeling?

No matter how you feel, we've all been there. Give yourself the space and grace to process and work through it.

A great strategy to use for yourself, your family or team is a two-word check-in. Give two words to describe how you're feeling. Ask your team members and family for two words too.

When someone says words like stressed, sad, uneasy, anxious, hesitant, scared, nervous, burned out, depressed or any other negative emotion, ask, "How can I help?"

There is a big difference to our brains between asking a question and making a statement.

If you say, "Let me know how I can help," chances are they won't let you know.

When you ask, "How can I help?" their brain is wired to answer the question. If they say, "I'm not sure," ask again, and they likely will answer.

This also lets them know that you care about them as a person and you really do want to help. They will feel seen and heard, which is what every human wants. Asking this simple question helps you form a stronger connection and deeper bond with the other person because you're meeting them with compassion, empathy, and understanding. And you're seeing them as a whole person.

Who can you reach out to today and ask, "How are you really feeling?"

You will make a lasting impact and might even save a life.

Bonus Tip 5: Say Yes to Adventures

Your definition of adventure might be different than that of your friends and/or family. If you ask 10 people what adventurous looks like to them, you'll get 10 different answers. **And this is about you.** Whatever your level or definition of adventure is, what is one microstep that will allow you to push your limits just a little bit?

You don't want it to be so far outside your comfort zone that you freeze just thinking about it. Then it's highly unlikely that you'll do it. Just gently nudge yourself outside what feels comfortable.

Here are a few ideas to get you started to Say Yes to adventures:

Hiking	Golfing
Sky diving	Entering a contest
Food trucking	Public speaking
Outdoor concert	Taking a class
Jet skiing	Renting an RV
Camping	Asking a stranger out on a date
New restaurant	Taking an improv class

Big or small, what's the next adventure you want to Say Yes to?

Bonus Tip 6: Say Yes to Relationships

The longer you're in relationships, whether professional or personal relationships, you tend to slide into your role and do the same things in the same way with the other person/people.

Spice up your relationships.

Have conversations about new topics. Ask out of this world questions. Dig deeper to get to know them on another level. Let down your guard. Develop more understanding, compassion, and empathy for them and allow them to develop it for you.

Keep them on their toes so they don't know what to expect, in the best possible way. Do something thoughtful or out of character. Plan an outing to somewhere they've always dreamed of going, even if it's not somewhere you really want to go, and watch their face light up with excitement.

How can you bring joy, laughter and fun into someone else's life?

Say Yes to being what the other person needs and you might discover it's exactly what you need too.

Bonus Tip 7: Say Yes to Professional Growth

A promotion might come along and you don't think you have all of the qualifications it asks for, apply anyway.

Someone wants to recommend you to a task force, but you aren't sure what it entails. Get on the task force anyway.

You're asked to move to a new city for work. Nothing is really holding you to your current city but you feel nervous, move anyway.

Stop talking yourself out of opportunities that are calling your name, and start talking yourself into doing them.

If you find yourself hesitating because you think you lack experience, aren't smart enough, don't have the right background, aren't leadership material or anything else, do it anyway.

Say Yes to the professional opportunities that come your way, even if you don't know how to do it. You'll find the help, resources or will power to figure it out.

What professional opportunity is open for you to Say Yes to?

Bonus Tip 8: Say Yes to Travel

Travelling is good for the soul.

When I travel, it allows me to slow down, take in the scenery and expand my mind to what is possible. I become a lot more curious, resourceful, and energized to explore.

Traveling allows me to learn about other people, cultures, and ways of life. It literally lights my soul on fire.

When you stay in what you know, it becomes natural to just do what the day calls for. Travelling allows you to stop, pause, and slow down which is good for your health.

Travel with an open mind and an open heart, and you'll find that you get what you want and also what you need in order to feel recharged and to keep showing up as your best you.

What will travelling do for you?

Where do you want to travel to next and what do you want to gain from the experience?

Bonus Tip 9: Say Yes to a Break

Saying Yes to a career break or sabbatical might be just what you need if you're feeling on the edge of burnout.

My friend and best-selling author of *Taking a Career Break for Dummies* Katrina McGhee says, "Sometimes, a long weekend just isn't enough to fully recover and recharge your batteries."

Saying Yes to a career break gives you the space to step back, relax, and think about your life without the stress of daily tasks and deadlines. You might discover the habits and thoughts that lead to burnout (If it's helpful, I have a book and resources on burnout), so you can make changes and avoid hitting burnout upon return.

If you're thinking about taking a career break, Katrina says start by figuring out why you **really** need it. Develop a purpose statement to consider why this break is important and what might happen if you don't take it.

Writing down your Why will help you see things more clearly, realize what's truly at stake (i.e your well-being!) and keep you motivated as you plan out your time away from work.

When you're interviewing for a job or negotiating your benefits, ask for a sabbatical after 3 or 5 years. These are becoming increasing popular. Companies are willing to give them because they don't want to lose their most valuable people, and they recognize the importance of wellness for you.

Set yourself up for success with a career break or a sabbatical by creating a plan. Plan out the length of time, what you want to do, and how much it's going to cost you (pro tip: it always cost more than you think, so it's better to save more).

Then have a guide for how to navigate your time away, as well as navigating your return. The last thing you want when you go back is to feel overwhelmed or stressed. Create a guideline for how you'll ease back into work and life (especially if you're traveling for long periods during your time off).

Saying Yes to a break in your routine may be the best thing for yourself.

How might a career break or sabbatical help you right now?

If you need some guidance or help, reach out to Katrina McGhee at KatringMcGheecoaching.com.

Bonus Tip 10: Become a Say Yeser

As you go through your journey of Saying Yes, you'll start to discover, uncover, and explore many more things you want to Say Yes to.

Become a Say Yeser, where you Say Yes to things just to try them, because you never know what you like until you try it.

First time you ever had pizza or a soda pop. Or rode your first roller coaster or traveled to a new city.

You didn't know if you would like them until you Said Yes to them.

Venture out from the sides, get in the middle and set your sails. You never know where they might take you.

Say Yes to things you never thought you'd do or always wanted to do. Never stop Saying Yes. You'll become who you were meant to be in the process.

The magic awaits. What will you Say Yes to next?

More

BONUS: DOWNLOAD YOUR FREE COPY OF THE SAY YES LIST

Are you ready to start your Say Yes Bucket List?

You're ready to turn your dreams or goals into reality and we're here to make it easy.

Download our free template that walks you through our step-by-step process to keep track of your Say Yes List items as well as the progress you're making.

When you don't know where or how to start, this is the perfect resource for you to begin turning your dreams and goals from impossible to possible and then to probable, turning them into reality. Whether it's a career, travel or love, if you want to turn it into the live you love, start now with our free download and watch your life transform before your eyes.

DOWNLOAD YOUR COPY OF THE EBOOK 101 WAYS TO SAY YES

Once you download your free Say Yes List template, you'll be given an option to get your copy of our ebook, which gives you 101 ways to Say Yes starting today.

If you've ever wanted to begin Saying Yes but just couldn't think of anything, we've got you covered.

Categorized into five different areas, this book shares lots of ways to Say Yes in your work, personal life, relationships, and with yourself. Wherever you want to Say Yes, this is a fantastic book that provides you with suggestions, and it's bound to spur more adventures, excitement and ideas within you. As you explore the book, you'll have a whole lot of fun!

SPEAKING

"Remarkable! Tremendous! Life Changing! You exceeded my expectations! You are truly an amazing motivational speaker, and I highly recommend you."
— Patti, meeting planner.

As seen on NBC for her work and research on burnout, Thought Leader **Jessica Rector** is known for her high energy, engaging, and entertaining keynote presentations.

With her fun, likeable personality and interactive style, she has the uncanny ability to immediately connect with audiences making her a memorable and in-demand speaker. Her rare combination of vulnerability, substance, and humor, while using her company's research to ignite people, performance, and profits will create change on the spot.

Audiences love her research, takeaways and the games they play during her sessions which allows her sticky content to create long-term results.

Through her company, Vitalize Unlimited, Jessica has worked with teams, leaders, and organizations like the Dallas Mavericks, ScotiaBank, and Tyler Technologies.

Jessica is a sure-fire win with audiences in any industry because she focuses on what makes us human. Then allows you to exceed your potential in business and life. She tailors all presentations to the needs of each unique audience.

Jessica inspiration transfers offstage, as her young son, Blaise Rector is also a sought after speaker, inspiring and motivation audiences to be their best selves in every role.

If you're looking for strong takeaways, audience interaction, and a lot of fun, book Jessica today (817) 523-1529.

TRAINING

Vitalize Unlimited is an all-in-one platform to prevent and beat burnout. This first to market product suite is designed to tackle the 5 key areas to improve employee experiences.

Jessica's team helps organizations improve performance, communication, and leadership all while reducing turnover, stress and burnout. Jessica specifically designs training, in person or online, for organizations who want their teams, staff or executives to move to the next level.

These solutions can be tailored into a half day, full day, monthly or longer sessions to fit your needs. In order to create massive change, it takes consistent learning. Jessica also offers video series for your people to continually learn, grow and improve.

CONSULTING

Jessica works with companies who want to create massive change. She helps organizations identify the impact of burnout on their organization, leaders, and employees' mental health and develops personalized programs to create happy, healthy, thriving workforces and cultures.

Since burnout affects various aspects of work and home lives, she tailors her consulting programs to each organization's objectives, ensuring everyone's needs are met from executives to employees.

She's known to create massive results that transfer to other departments, improving bottom-line results and employee well-being throughout the organization.

FOR MORE INFORMATION:

For speaking inquiries, training or consulting, please go to
jessicarector.com

or call Jessica directly at (817) 523-1529

One-stop-shop product suite to prevent and beat burnout while enhancing mental health:
go to VitalizeUnlimited.com

Tame Your Brain Game: 52 Tips to Turn Negative Thoughts into Positive Action

In this transforming book, Jessica Rector, a thought leader on self-talk, walks you through your negative thoughts and how their impacting your life and gives you strategies to turn them into positive action for better results. Your inner conversations, what you say to yourself about yourself, is the foundation for everything in your life, at work, and in relationships. Jessica gives you proven steps, which have helped thousands, to take action and create massive change. These tips work for anyone, anytime, and anywhere. If you're ready to improve your work, relationships, and life, uplevel yourself or create a change, no matter how big or small, this is a must-have book. Get your copy today!

Blaze Your Brain to Extinguish Burnout: 52 Keys to Prevent, Break Through and Extinguish Burnout

Burnout is the #1 reason why people leave organizations, and it's not going away anytime soon. That's where Jessica comes in.

Burnout impacts every industry, company and team, but it doesn't have to be that way. Through a decade of research, Jessica Rector shares the 20 contributing factors of burnout, what leaders must do to prevent it, and the best strategies to implement to keep burnout away in her #1 Best-Selling book. It's no longer "a nice to have" to address burnout; it's a must have.

Get your copy today to help your company, leaders, and team with the biggest issue impacting the workforce.

The Adventures of B Man: Blaise Your Brain

Five-year-old Blaise, aka B Man, takes you on the fun and enlightening ride in his first book. He motivates, inspires, and empowers you to life a life you enjoy, while having the courage to be yourself.

This book, the first in the series, became a #1 best-seller within minutes of being published. Adults and kids alike are learning, growing, and transforming from taking to heart and implementing the tips B Man shares in this one-of-a-kind book.

Join B Man as he takes you through fun, excitement and a lot of laughs that only he can do. So, buckle up, put on your cape, and enjoy the wild ride with The Adventures of B Man. Get Ready to Blaise Your Brain!

The Adventures of B Man: Blaise a Trail

As a follow up to his popular first book, The Adventures of B Man: Blaise Your Brain, now six-years-old, Blaise, B Man, embarks on more adventures.

In this #1 best-selling book, B Man guides you through life lessons and perspectives that every kid (and adult) needs to hear or be reminded of in order to find more joy, happiness, and love, while also exploring the opportunities for fun. You're bound to learn, grow and gain a lot of wisdom and insight, because sometimes kids have a lot to teach us.

As B Man will tell you, there are always lots of opportunities for more fun, and sometimes they only take a minute or two.

Come along, as B helps you explore those small moments that will transform your life.

Breaking the Silence: Taking the SH(hh) Out of Shame-#1 Best-Selling Book

"Powerful, insightful, and life changing! Jessica helps you get to the core of what's holding you back from more confidence and success. This book is a must read for anyone who is ready for an extraordinary life."— Chris Widener, NYT Best-Selling Author

In this ground-breaking #1 best-selling book, Jessica Rector takes you on a journey to uncover how shame is holding you back at work and home and what it takes to create a solid foundation on which to create a life you love. In just five steps, from recognizing shame to knowing how to confront it when it comes up again, Jessica gives you a blueprint for lasting results. This book helps you release your shame, speak your voice, and stand in your power.

Life Defining Moments From Bold Thought Leaders- #1 Best-Selling Book

"Make your trip to a great life infinitely easier by reading, absorbing, and obtaining all the best that life offers. It helps you have more love, joy, and fulfillment by living your life passionately on-purpose." — Mark Victor Hansen, Co-Creator of World's Best-Selling Book Series, Chicken Soup for the Soul

In this #1 best-selling book, Jessica Rector demonstrates pure vulnerability when she shares her life-altering story that found her into the depths of despair. She guides you through her journey of how it propelled her into transforming the lives of others, speaking on stages to thousands, and living her mission. Jessica was able to turn her pain into something bigger and empowers you to do the same.

Live Your Greatest Life Book

"This book shows you how to unleash your full potential for love, health, happiness, and complete fulfillment in life." — Brian Tracy, Motivational Speaker and author of *Change Your Thinking, Change Your Life*

Through the six steps to living the life you've always wanted, this book guides you to step out of your rut, get out of your own way, and leap to your future. Through real world examples it inspires you to reach your potential.

Through a step-by-step processes Jessica helps you increase your self-confidence, love yourself, and become your authentic self, by finding your passion, confronting your fears, and exploring what you really want in life. This empowering guide has shown thousands of people the tools and techniques to make the change they need to thrive, and it will for you too. Get this book and achieve your goals and dreams today!

Live Your Greatest Life Journal

Create change and take massive action fast, when you know how to move forward. Writing is one of the most therapeutic and liberating things you can do for yourself. Sometimes you just don't know the questions to ask yourself to get unstuck or to make forward progress.

This journal guides you each step of the way. It asks you the tough questions, most you probably don't know to ask yourself, and gives you the space to find your way to the answers.

Bottling your thoughts up just holds you back, so this journal allows you to release them in an organized and fluid way.

With this journal, you will dig deep, stretch yourself, and make forward progress through the Live Your Greatest Life book faster while keeping track of your thoughts, ideas, and goals.

The BS Quote Book
Breaking The Silence: Taking The Sh(hh) Out Of Shame Quote Book

The BS Quote Book shares some of the BS you tell yourself that holds you back and how to change it to get what you want most.

Sometimes we need that extra push, motivation, or inspiration to get us through or the reiteration that "I'm not the only one."

This mini book is ideal for that and has the best of the best thoughts, quotes, and lessons from the best-selling book *Breaking the Silence: Taking the Sh(hh) Out of Shame.* It's perfect to put it in your pocket or purse, send as a gift, or hand out to inspire others.

This book is often bought in bulk to share as a gift for team members, clients, or friends.

This Man Thing Quote Book

For, about, and with men from all over the world.

Start your day off right with wise, powerful insights from This Man Thing Quote Book. Inspired by a group of men who want to empower and motivate other men to keep showing up as their best selves in every aspect of their lives.

This mini book is filled with empowering advice, feedback, and lessons to help men through challenges, issues, or struggles and helps alleviate depression, anxiety and trauma. This book was created in hopes it might help, support and transform the lives of millions of men.

It is perfect for you or the men in your life as a gift, to inspire others or to keep in your pocket for daily inspiration.

This book is often bought in bulk to share as a gift for team members, clients, or friends.

ABOUT THE AUTHOR

Jessica Rector's mission is simple: Transform Lives.

As the top burnout expert and Founder of Vitalize Unlimited, the first of its kind products suite to prevent burnout, Jessica is the authority on tackling your inner game and turning it into outer success and positive action!

Jessica's journey started with just an idea and the belief in herself, which has now transformed thousands of lives to get out of their comfort zone and keep being their amazing, best selves.

Jessica is known for her rare combination of enthusiasm, energy, and entertainment making her a dynamic, Must-See presenter. Whether they're playing a game or doing the "Who's a ROCKSTAR" activity, audiences love her because she's innovative, impactful, and interactive, often considered the best at the conference.

As a former TV talk show host and an award winning #1 top sales performer at a Fortune 100 company, Jessica knows firsthand how to turn your thoughts into massive business and life results. She uses her company's research, experiences, and strategies to help organizations, leaders, and teams fire up their thinking, extinguish burnout, and ignite their people while having more fun.

Jessica has three college degrees, including an MBA, and has written 12 books. As a #1 best-selling author, some of her clients include Sociabank, the Dallas Mavericks, and Fortune's Best Company to Work for. Jessica has been seen on NBC, Dr. Phil's Merit Street, ABC, and CBS, for her research and work on burnout.

Jessica enjoys learning about the exciting world of Transformers so she can carry on real conversations with her son, Blaise, a #1 best-seller author, motivational speaker and her CFO, Chief Fun Officer.

Vitalize Unlimited's purpose is to help 50 million people prevent and beat burnout and enhance mental health. They work with companies, leaders, teams and individuals in their one-stop-shop product suite. They are first to market with a platform that encompasses everything burnout related.

They also have a buy one, give one model. For every one purchased, they give another one to a non-profit doing good things in the world. If you want to purchase this one-of-a-kind platform for your company, team or self, please go to VitalizeUnlimited.com.

If you would like to put your non-profit on the list to receive a "give one," please email us at info@VitalizeUnlimited.com.

For speaking engagements, training or consulting, please go to JessicaRector.com for more information.

Contact us at Jessica@JessicaRector.com and (817) 523-1529.

Made in the USA
Middletown, DE
26 June 2024